Now Chiefly Poetical

— BOOKS BY KEVIN DI CAMILLO —

Of The Hovrs (1997)

Why I Drive Alfa Romeos (& Other Excuses) (1997)

Yours (& Others) (1999)

John Paul II in the Holy Land: In His Own Words
(Editor, with Rev. Lawrence Boadt) (2005)

NOW CHIEFLY POETICAL

KEVIN DI CAMILLO

BLAZEVOX[BOOKS]
Buffalo, New York

NOW CHIEFLY POETICAL
by Kevin Di Camillo

Published by BlazeVOX [books]

Interior design and typesetting by Geoffrey Gatza
Cover Art by Mark Dellas, 2001

First Edition
ISBN: 978-1-60964-294-5
Library of Congress Control Number: 2017944649

BlazeVOX [books]
131 Euclid Ave
Kenmore, NY 14217

Editor@blazevox.org

publisher of weird little books

BlazeVOX [books]

blazevox.org

21 20 19 18 17 16 15 14 13 12 01 02 03 04 05 06 07 08 09 10

BlazeVOX

For Alicia
El raemanso de tu boca
Bajo espesura de besos
(Lorca)

“But the law of love is not concerned with what will be, what ought to be, what can be. Love does not reflect; it is unreasonable and knows no moderation. Love refuses to be consoled when its goal proves impossible, despises all hindrances to the attainment of its object. Love destroys the lover if he cannot obtain what he loves; love follows its own promptings and does not think of right and wrong. Love inflames desires which impel it toward things that are forbidden. But why continue?”

—Saint Peter Chrysologus, c. 450

«Ich hätte gerne ein gutes Buch hervorgebracht. Es ist nicht so ausgefallen; aber die Zeit ist vorbei, in der es von mir verbessert warden könnte. »

“I should have liked to produce a good book. This has not come about, but the time is past in which I could improve it.”

—Ludwig Wittgenstein, *Philosophical Investigations*

Contents

Part III

Part IV

FOREWORD

KEVIN DI CAMILLO'S poems are so finely tuned that they risk calling the reader's attention too exclusively to their form and to all the fragile echoes from other writers that haunt them. But the risk is taken with a degree of deliberateness, because the poems keep revealing, within the cadences of American speech, a ritual foundation. This is apparent in their pace-- free and easy for the most part but every so often caught in the coils of a heavier feeling, delayed into slow motion. The effect is that the poems become meditations without ever becoming too solemn. They are somber, although the speaking voice can vary-- even waver-- from anger to humour, and the tonal music is complex, and has many different hues. NOW CHIEFLY POETICAL is choral in its effects, constantly bringing the lyric solo flights back into the harmonies of a stern but consoling communal order.

This volume is, in itself, plotted as a complicated sequence, and is not merely a gathering of incidental or occasional poems. The opening lyric poems are immediately arresting; but it is in the retrospect afforded them by the "Gradual Psalms" and the Stations of the Cross that they fully reveal themselves. The sequence is in some respects simple— it starts with an account of the world and of the way it has been glimpsed in various writers; then the transience of this is absorbed into the meditative sequences that follow, although the absorption of one world into another is a painful one; then it is celebrated in the Joycean epithalamium.

This is poetry of the highest order, deserving of wide recognition.

SEAMUS DEANE
Dublin

ACKNOWLEDGEMENTS

I am grateful to the following journals and their editors who first published the following poems:

"Air: Fin." in The Antigonish Review, spring 2008, issue 151.

"Were All There", Daedalus: Journal of the American Academy of Arts & Sciences, Vol.135, issue 4 - fall 2006

from "The Gradual Calm: part CXXI", Opium, www.opiumden.org, November 25, 2007, http://www.opiummagazine.com/Index.aspx?storyid=1160.

from "The Gradual Calm: parts CXXIV and CXXVII", Opium, www.opiumden.org, August 28, 2008, http://www.opiummagazine.com/Index.aspx?storyid=1160

from "The Gradual Calm: part CXXXIV", Prairie Fire, spring 2007, Vol. 28, number 1.

from "The Gradual Calm: part CXXXV", The Bend, spring, 2006, number 3.

from "The Gradual Calm: part CXXII", The National Poetry Review, spring/summer 2005, Vol. 3, number 1.

from "The Gradual Calm: part CXXIII", Italian Americana, winter 2000,Vol. XVIII, number 1.

"July 4", James Joyce Quarterly, spring 1999, Vol. 36, number 3.

"The Beautiful Monk", Notre Dame Review, fall 1999, number 8.

Now Chiefly Poetical

I

Can't go on w/ this—
Can't go on w/ this unless—
I go on w/ you

The Beautiful Monk

In a shaft of panic was he
not dreaming
being other

the what was thought
to unravel
the constant knot

being woven madness
her distaff
no pastor's crozier up

-side-down
spinning a replicate. No, not
now. Easy *Nones* where he trod

discalceated (I hate
& I hate that, too) unaware
of the cold coal priest

-collar-white,
those. And like I say he was

for Sam Turner

Were All There

The seller of used-cars, his cigar
noisome, quasi-Cuban; the nuncio
in his scrim of pallium: didn't cough.
The neverseen neighbour (gay?)
who stopped to say he was "sorry".
Monsignor-the-trencherman
& his Romanic subdeacons with
collection nets on poles, horizontal
gondoliers with monstrous patens.
The Smiths, wizards, women; Children
cursed by the undertaker & his
stained presence; Keeners; Common
& Collect; The old friend
with his index cards (too large)
ready to play apologist.
The rest of it.

for Geoffrey Hill

Night Spent By Area Man

On the web
In the net
His cell filled
w/ candles, hand

As in Daniel
Writing on magic
Screen: caveats &
Unctuous e-misses:

She misses him.
We all miss someone
(not him) or else
something is

wrong w/ this
ill-limned
stilled-life in-
stallation: his eyes

empty as Lucy's,
are now olives
in an old
fashioned sidecar

he removed from
the dusty teak
(possibly oak)
sideboard. He's bored

--says to himself—
slurs, rather, slurs
a letter
he should answer

(he calls bills
"letters": it sounds
so much better)
He feels now

So much better:
Listen to that
Trash-man—is
He singing?! Holy

Fuck! Clock ticks.
Cat's ticks stock up
On Sam (he's the
Cat). Clock

Tocks. It's five.
That makes this
Morning technically.
Bed-time for the

Area man whose
Dominion vanishes
While galaxies expand
Like clock coils

Sprung open & out.
Let out Sam.
Let in Sun.
Let *Vigils* come

& go in
silence. Go to
Bed, he says.
So he goes to

Bed w/ another
wasted night
On his head. He
Goes to bed.

Keep a
sleep
a wake
is no place
to dream

Compline Complaint

"Shorter are the prayers in bed. But more heart-felt" -Rilke

Après "Kyrie, Christe,
Kyrie"--   see: I'm
sorry,   swear.
Where?
There?   'k.

Intoned, off-keyed *nunc dimittis*: for
us   it
is   orison,
oblation
for the dark side of the   sun.
Given,
becomes
your spikenard's splendid reek:
took one week to rid the shards of   that smashed
jar, the floor a field of infinitesimal
moon crescents, toenails: the balm
has blown
& your hair dries, feels
not unlike sin
w/ redemption inclusive. Rip the interdict into this—
so cold the   terminus
was
ridiculous: absolute zero
on all meters, mercury dropped like
solder: one crement
not malleable
slow as a wheel-chair marathoner
w/ one good arm, one
gone
for good.
Desire? To thank.
Hope   to thank while

exhaling much fog
w/ the hope and desire all along.

for Katie Kamphuis

4ß

Emptied symbols
dented cymbals,
timbrels--
                    so long

back from centre
for the memory.
Let me.
                    Wrong

87%.
Bed's ledge needs a
ruler: 2 ft.
                    Phyrrhic

noise, like gathering
of rough cord on worn
oak core
                    polished past

luster, burnished
like a porcelain
crucible in melting
                    furnace

where they pass,
unburnéd, those
three wise
                    sons,

their song sung
comfortably—too
much to say
                    anyway

here it is, the balled
result of
unwound
                    twine

on hands, so untied,
ununited, tied to
nothing but
                    eachother

together. It never works
out but in prayer there
is even an answer
                    to cancer:

No surprise it starts w/ an
"L"—ice-tong quotation-
marks pick letter like angle:
                    Lean into it.

Melancholic Litany

Go to work. Stay home.
Get dressed. Rest in bed.
Breakfast? Drink instead.
        It can't possibly matter.

Call her, apologise. Fuck her.
Fix flat. Forget that chore.
Change locks. Let doors go.
        It can't possibly matter.

Write her. Don't write ever.
Re-read letters. Throw in fire.
Stare at pictures. Feed to scissors.
        It can't possibly matter.

Move to New York. Stay here.
Take that job. Take leave.
Leave me alone. Visit my ward.
        It can't possibly matter.

for Dick Allen

Pôme, Get Well

And for all that
the world's not
spent
yet
went
w/ it, the casualcausal
touch

locus
(putatively per accidens)—
When? ca. 2
AM—ah!

Elisha, when Xanax blues
come in, it's better than [blank]
or drinks. CALL TIME
AGAIN, KEEPER,
thô we've invested Goldman-Sachs
in the jukebox
our selections rock
(but the volume sucks). Then unplug, cut
lights, pull
the metal shutters
which look like half-turned gutters
over glassless windows.
Imply

insist that we leave

(please).
So the sts & aves @ the end of SoHo
were we there then-- of
a sudden, a catarrh from
yer lung like a guitar string's
spontaneous break & coil
sent your pectoral cross

starting from skin to oxygen
(& back again) to breast
bone, its base. Left alone
I was, with images of yer slip
into fever under Hudson in
Holland, where floods are
norm—didn't touch, but
looked warm—all while
remonstrating w/ self:

She gathers flowers,
She changes.

75 Channels

My cousin, he works for the cable company--
I get my cable for free:
HBO, Skinemax, E!,
ESPN-- all of
them come into my
den for nothing just like
ABC, NBC, FOX
or CBS
I guess. And there's never
anything on--
thô there's
nothing wrong w/ my set:
it's as if I'm blind
to what's correct in minor

matters
(e.g.: does a fork stay on a cleared plate at a restaurant?)
I don't know.
I don't know what
I want besides a dish-- not for
more
TV, but
to let the
neighbours
see me on the roof,
mounting
that half-shell
as if on
Venus, trying to catch a signal
from earth:

Houston: this is Kevin.
Do you read me
Over? And over?

To Me

All the rest were
others
to be
endured. Please send
your tome
home
to me.
To be
or not
to be: *is* that a question?
Whomever may
explain
attraction
may explain it
away.
Say: all cricket
players spoke no English;
the crickets themselves squeaked
sex through legs through sheer
limb-friction; a limpid ray dripped so clear--
not fixity

not stasis

but an

open
window for the dark-looker to climb through
into
your slack mouth-- till
wakened

when paralyzed jaw
is all
trismus
& tongue gone with the gold-bug slave. Don't fret

yet:
I'll
get
the salve. I still
have it.

Legion's Elision

And thô it seems same, Sam,
                    As Albany's sad rivers
          (avoid obvious rime—one word
titles & capitals, especially when the word
          is recondite, turn poems into
definitions)-- carpal and metacarpus
blackgloved in humus (in long work, try
          not to end w/ beginning, V. late Hill).
That is not for you (this). Avoid that.
                    Why Kentucky Colonels were stripped
(1950s) only to be recomissioned 1 month later,
Jeremias? What happened to The Cardinal's
2d laureate?
                    Duodenum to
                         Rectum is ruined: heatsheafs
Devoured in the oven's cellar, a so-so inferno—
Meant "S.O.S. Oh, D'inverno", cold as Hecht. Swore
To give lives for even
                A rayon mozzetta, thô rainwrecked, more
                                                  Net than
                                                  Not. Signor
Mazzotta called one of the Seami "American": wrote,
Asked Ecco = a "note e veloce". (Never "Nice was
                                             'Nice'"). But
There I was, limicolous, fucivorous & nonplussed—
Sentensed for serial offings thurified & demi-
Merged to the teraphim & the PMOY 1999AD. Like
Multure to mine own mill whilst thine swain ate paine
Demaine—caught by this apparatchik: so played
          We swived. I swithe   still: near year-aged
Fronds flamed till ash—too close. And the offered
          Raccolta in censer's furnace. Hands
          Hurt—Quit! Admit!: Burned as acolyte
(avoid the incondite) in winter, when Sir Father

returned the—first Mass—the calefactory, that is
pome.   Underwrote this
  one.

The Jesse Tree

Do you know that I wish your fingers were flowers?
Every picture would find you proffering bouquets
Which could never be thrown. So much scent! Those colours
More than mere film can record with its chameleon-grey
That goes with nothing. Yes, there are other things I wish:
For your head to turn to marble, your hair to oil;
Your arms to ivy-vines, legs to saplings, feet to fish;
The whole of your body coated in a clear golden foil.
All your transmorphications! All of them I'd love
As surely as if you came in hot from mowing the lawn
To reveal two of your fingers cut by a careless move
Of hand near blade. Or if your eyes burst during a yawn.
"Impossible!" you state and leave shaking your head.
You're right. But I wish you were something else instead.

Etched Deruta

Endless aisles, infinite
unutile, centreless shapes—
like you, Spaniard,
aboard the davenport
in the portico-entrance—
seated, leaning (somewhat
stuffed) on the sofa

in the gathering Limbo
chapel—pre-credo,
poetry of preëverything (no
opening acclamation) in
your eyes shone
a long, lone Paschal candle
in Barcelona's grotto

where I carved out
your aorta, branding a
crux, vessel-fashioned, hemo-
globin implosion—
the orbit of your
iris, pupil's circle,
lancerated w/out tear.

Care for you, Spaniard—
ejaculations jammed with
piety at the altar of
the God-blesséd Lord, before
the hand-turned tabernacle
door, spending frankincense
like talents, sealing opened

unguents & ashes plashed
w/ light from varigated
windows, a hole
for the heart, the cœur's

trench, a furrow spiration
clean-filled, leveled. Now
stand on it, discalced.

The End of Bethany

From the broken, halved
garnet protruding from a worn
jamb hung
one brined blanket
wrung with sand.

And no one ever came to claim it.

II

The Gradual Calm:
a song of the steps

I: [Complimentary Degrees of Ascension]

CXX

At loss for suitable malediction: treacherous |
tongue (bless none
theless) of strangers—embered coals | on shoal
off-shore.

Sempiternal September's nocturnal fire from | cedar
driftwood, brushwood, all night angling:
completely nothing. | Could fell
the bo, too, jackself | in jack-

boots: aloof, a lonely denizen, Cain I | am and
aim for (believe in me)
Peace, *vox pax*. But just words they are.
| Have
none of that—
want pugilist for psalmist. When I hit you | you're it,
no backs ∞. | What
said, just said? Regardless, I did live w/
malefactors |for what

seemed like forever.
Again, it's what I deserved and I deserve a lot |worse.

CXXI

I to the cairn: "S.O.S.!" Not
"Song of Songs". No. Our souls.

From the artificer, sap-soled | insomniac w/ his pince-nez,
cigaret-holder, rod-drawn | dual-monocled maniac. Perfect
postured poseur, sheathed in | ultraviolet radiation & lunar
illumined. Like a Pinkerton |sleepwalking rounds through
primed *Lauds,* going & coming,
shading.

CXXII

House? S'open
        gate, a guard.
Wigwam: content
        w/in this cone
tent, a throne sent
        from Rome
meant the resident's
        home shone
w/ the bones bent
        into ornament
of the fence rent
        once as gate
lent passage:
        peace & welcome!
Along w/: *fast & repast!*
        In your teepee
city, may the dove's
        descent, the pigeon's
descant fall like walls
        of Berlin, Jericho,
China, & I don't know...
        Buffalo? Let them
down, invisible as Paul
        at night thru wall
cum lintel. Dove's call:
        mind cauled w/
fortunate portent: dom
        -ionions down like dom
-inoes & exploded
        cathedrals: Rheims,
Cologne—did the dome
        of Saint Paul's go?
No. Then as I do, benedict
        me so: from high
as the high-ridged, mighty
        mountains of Bashan
may peace rain from sky

like manna in Cana
          w/ vino for H_2O. Did some
one say “Amen”?
          Then do it again, w/
meaning. I mean it.

CXXIII

Lift, Atlas, eyes in
dish like Lucia—
I see a slave who
stares at his man's

hands. The servant
glares at mistress
like looking for him,
Mister Jones, in

manifold hiding
places. Come now,
come down now,

bow low to ground
at base of Hill's praise
& lament. Streams
in brooklets pocked

by rain *o lavabo me*:
may I be clean w/
mammon for manna
while suckling like

Romulus & Remus
who were only Able—go
on, sue me for libel. Here's
your sequel to the Bible.

CXXIV

If—

            our song...

If—

            our song...

Then
one of the following:

like first-time water
w/ mouth in love, ostiated,
capacious-- swallowed
us till skin sallowed
as an old tome in dormer.
Having followed, they
swept us, drowning in
waves of enemies:
good-bye.

Are wingèd words darts?
Returned, their waters on
fire in the pyre of pulled-
out pilings. Flight like
birds darting from arrows,
like a sparrow expert in
springing from a nest
suddenly a mess, in
distress from battery
by a battalion of archers
marching past, in flight,
through a wall of wave
curling a pipeline, a
horizontal whirlpool closes
conically, unslaked, for
having flown, the sparrow,
spared by the bow, can
see who made the sea

& left it hungry: hence, she
sings doxology.

CXXV

Ensconced city in mountains ranged
w/ a love, capped in blanched
sentiment: *o urbi*, stay surrounded
by ardour, forevermore.

The feral, infernal hirelings perambulate,
reconnoiter your daughter—she
is oblivious. It's dangerous to live like this,

to be so. Then don't go. Stay & sit & sew:
steal father's cincture, let the metropolitan's
silken mantle bell-out like a carillon's canon

rending silence like long gauze caught
in a saw's single jaw, always
open, forever tetanussed. Stay apertured

& awake. May those who dœvil
never prevail. But on us:
Regnum Dei intra vos.

CXXVI

Manacles fall from phalanges and manus
like gravity's gaining on the horizon, taking
on the sun at Aphelion.
A loss of banded-hands
& a mouth all laughter: the song of psalms.

Say "YHWH". Is that any way to pray?

How to sew w/out a needle,
 w/a camel in the eye
of your brother, or a dromedary
 pregnant in mine own.

Deliver us, C.O.D., G-o-d, like a
 strip of creek in a desert, rain
dropped in sandbox that falls
 like glass hours.

Left office with a tear intersecting eye.
After happy hour, returned w/ smile
where copywritten-scowl once was scrawled.

CXXVII

To construct w/out a gardener
Is to dissemble a chimney
From smoke-spout down--
Cast its bricks through black
Shaft to draft & drown
In the grate fire.

More-- more than the blackened
Beefeater who scouts on
Spy Wednesday have I
Memorized your lines,
Mesmerized by eyes
Knotted as birch-skin
Red or white: on hands,
The stripes ripe & vesseled;
Twixt ribs, scraped skin
On tabula rasa of back
As foolscap.

Not dream-mare but fare
For the exhausted insomniac:
Bed early, no sleep deity
To make dreams reality--
To even dream of sleep,

Of children in a quiver,
Hand-picked by the warrior
Who smiles like a forest
Fire & stands under the
Scarlet torii unashamed,
Arguing happily w/ all
His family & enemies.
He smiles whenever
He looks at me.

CXXVIII

Parapathetic beatified on *via Dei.*
Repeat refrain again
ora et labora
A mendicant's chant, chanson
sing-along!
What I sew I eat
& wear: I'm a vine
replanted nine times
ninety times, banded,
grafted: a single
stem finger-thick
w/ signet ring
filleted to all walls
in my home, abode
where table is altared
& each meal a bloody
sacrifice of some life
or other's. My wife,
the fecund, rotund one,
round ever, tends winded
vines w/ braids & coiled
seraphs, plus hemi-hidden
worms which never die
& grubs, along w/ one
lone snail that trails
itself out-- a sugar comette—
from its coiled shell, coats
stems in –cose, lets them draw
all oils out, bleeds a cheap
unguent.

And the word from
the one to come:
(none to speak of, see above).

Even from this generation, back
past atavistic ancestry, still:
laetare et gaudete.
These days, these days
& evenings, out-stretched
like a tolled chasuble: spring
out the eremite in his homuncular
cellar, have him over
for supper, & on James, Seamus, Jacques
& Jacob: *pax in perpetuum*,
now, if not ever.

II: [The Later Middot]

CXXIX

Since infants
can't talk in
Latin, declaim:
Since infant stateus
what have they done
but
hung over us a pall, put
the pall in pallium,
pulled the
pall over us,
over our heads, this
mock-surplice, w/ a surfeit of furrows
borrowed from flogs burrowed in back
where precipitation ran red from cord's
marrow when ægis w/ a sparrow device
was cut up & down by master gardener's
shears, immense as Dali's scissors
in a spellbound dreamscape.

So scattered like migrant farmers'
seed may they be carelessly
solarised like stray blades,
incipient in a fakéd spring.
Stigmatatize their palms
so no produce nor coin may they
contain: arms emptied egg
shells, testicles unfilled & held
in OT covenant by an enemy's
hirsute hand.
A valediction? Just spit
in their direction.

CXXX

Sheol is sheer hell.
Who has ears to hear
                    here? Every
blemish marked, counted
& told to one whose belled
& burning rochet
can't stand, has no
leg to stand on
                in quicksand on
top of it, under feet all is
slowsand, growing to a
sullied ocean from
sendimental delta.

Waited for entry as if nailed
in the narthex.
Password? Which door is out,
which INRI?
More than the watchman
waits for dawn
have I longed for the password
from the passlord, the key
to all theologies, his skeleton
key: Px & IHS, desolate
& desiccating in his transfixed
tree: body makes a "T",
life copies alphabet. Reflect.
Genuflect. Interpret: What
will it profit you, prophet, if
you gain the world but bruise
your soul? Empurpled, emptied
emperor, your throne of melting gold.

Spring day breaks the day star.

CXXXI

Eyes—not up—too above, sublime, sublunary sufferance
of the quotidian which is enough for, caressed on the lap
of the matroness I was (I guess) content, more or less.

CXXXII

Naked, anxious king:
somnambulant, restive
w/in feckless litter, looks
for throne, cathedra, an ark—
where heard of? Found
in the Jar Field.
          No sleep, no rest for
temples till the king's emperor,
his despot-overlord has domiciled
in resting-place in piece-meal
chain-mail, under pisces, a fish-sleep.

The sprouting hour grew
like thorns on a rose-stem,
rose then on the mountain
where unseen sage king
chose his abode. Those
who opposed his elevation,
slain in their sheets now
shrouds for all, save the
cymarred in the forefront,
dining on meat & bread,
their way led by virgins—
not vestal, but w/al—
sans veils: stepped into
the jet evening, following
the gleam of the corolla
illumined on the calvarus
of the king's emperor's over
-seer on Mount Zion, where
schism was sewn back-together
w/ the thread of chrism.

CXXXIII

Not sweat
but dew running
down forehead to stew
on jaw's shadow.
Omnipotent ointment
oiling sandpaper-jowled
priests & Levites.

Not mist, not rain—balance—
between condensation
& condescension
of the rain-deity.

Sweet as rivulets from
The Episcopate's thumb
rubbed on forehead instead
of ashes, opaque Weds
emblem, brooking
(back in mind) into Father's
beard, ruining collar
in rust-colour.

The cataract's veil of mist
refreshes as cold cloud
crowning Hermon & Zion.

A thurifer's tiara, on the
chalkéd ground-- the damp
moss for us a sort of solace.

CXXXIV

Clear glottis, choir: no victim
of slumber be among your
members. Night hours, named
& numbered, rank as
unfilled blanks in Breviary.
Keep brief, then, this
unexegetical exhortation—
blackwatched-plaid clan: Watch!

W/ lifted hands free
from all
anxiety: free for all (not
in body, by Paul) those
who come w/ baked palettes
& tongues wrung saliva-dry.
From tor-top, a benediction
on the choir who wait
more for the Lord than
for daybreak. So, more
for weariness of life, not love
of Thee: bless me. Please.
O, priests & Levites, Elvis
& anchorites—bless & be blessed—
leave me w/ doxology.

III

Watch Your Step-sister

"Grant us, outside of sleep, serenity." – Seferis.

Residue of pastel pasted
w/ fixative taints nail
& fingertip. The arches

are aching for insoles.
The Seminoles are screaming
for the chief must be

renamed. Yer departure:
like 8 lb.-test bunched
in my throat, the lure

hooks from larynx to deep
G/I. Why no smell reminds.
Why no one is in this bldg.

Bringing ice in that afghan—
Can't fall for sleep in a net so
deep & loaded, thô

readied for a monsooned
pic-nic. Toothpicks prepped
for that immaculate gap

one loves to tongue.

Not ill because
Not at all.

Cable the captain: the capstan
is jammed w/ used bandage, film
& ribbands.

Ban the baragouin: they
make me keen
like a Belfasted siren.

It always only grows
recursive: of course, Jer,
I know you know who sends it:
were you not the Minister
of Franking Privileges on that
island never to have been discovered?

O! For the genius of self-irrigation.
Felt like that one   just then
there was unbroken quiet   in heaven
for about ½ an hour.

Nocturne: On

When
can I see you
again? My
eyes have perfect ∞/∞
vision
when you're
in
them.

2 x 4

So not
Worth it.
    Serenade the daysleeper,
    Walking in sound:
    Debates the remuneration
    Of lying down (again).

So what
Is it?
    Am all wrong. Brings back
    That song, an artefact
    Of a juvenile insomniac.
    Re-strain that lay.

To what
Purpose?
    ¼ x 4 over unslept hours.
    Re-read that *Quarterly*:
    they just won't publish me.
    Love the new cover. Clever.

Are you
Tired yet?
    Yes, as an ecdysiast bores
    Of cold, maybe a sliver of
    Shame. Pointless pills on
    Floor or in gullet: no difference.

So this
Then, right?
    Or wrong, am all. Sciolist
    In nascent winter's blanked
    Night; conjecture for
    Vocation or a ball-score.

And lay
Of love?
        The boss said that if he were
        The priest—but never heard
        The rest. Asti w/ Joey on Fire Is.
        Zöe mouthing sand like King's hay.

The test
To take?
        And rest I cannot make. Alas, can't
        Pass what won't serve. The Charter
        House is hot now; prior wears no cross,
        Thô he carries an awkward Jerusalem.

The space
Is short.
        Bud Court was great. But I might die
        Tonight, right—Trouble—all that. Was
        Great. But that was 88 Olds: stayed up
        & out until we saw the thawing Lake.

Talking Leaves

People leave during
the reading
of poems.
People come
to end the poetry
reading. They (the
audience) agree
to do The Wave
Good-bye.

for Kevin Patrick Corbett

The Dedications Keep Changing!
(Who Keeps Changing the Dedications?)

For my rough God
Jackboot-trodden, Molotovian
Explosion. (I do it
            w/out music).

A Styrian sings of a lemon
Tree, whose fruit she
Eats as oranges.

Trying to live
w/ your birthday
On Christmas.

A prayer after
Disaster (Ps. 60): deep-rest
& depressed under cypress, ink
of the olive press run
thru tresses, humming undressed
w/ clenched thirst in throat's
tundra: it's understood my
                                    high
ground is an eroding bluff.

For the least tincture of love

Whilst the viaduct
Looked like dawn.

The quarry where cutters swam
In mire. Later, embers in
Mouldering bonfire pit. A cliff
Sudden as an escapologist's
Opacity. The puff of pine,
Perfect haiku moment:

To rest, I'm so tired
To be buried in soft earth
To rest I'm so tired

"Jonah that stupid ark
-building fuck".

The satraps won't sit
For that. There
Are no chairs, only stairs
Where one cannot rest
Lest they be cast
Undersoled and smashed,
Breath no longer asked for.

It's Him! At the door!

Hilltop
or
A Poem for Harpsichord, Perhaps

Dinner and a movie is
A job. To work on. For
Money. I'm not from
Here, but here are some

Directions. Incredibly
Short notice—we waited
And waited. My apologies.
I'll try to explain it

Tomorrow. Or Later. Give
Me a page. Or a piece
Of paper. This message
is too long. I'm sorry

Apologies are again in
Order. As are the papers.
And the pages: please
Answer. When you can.

You must be busy. Or
Eating. Or sleeping.
The logistics have changed.
I'm not from here so

I can't say where, exactly,
You should be. You should
Be answering my pages.
And returning my calls.

Please. I'm not from here.
I don't know the area. And
The logistics have changed—
I can't say whether for better

Or not. But there it is.
Please page me
And remember to
Press pound.

for Alan McIntyre Smith

O You Were

born for this cathedra
    & the sycophantic hydræ
    of Secretariats, prothonotary
    apostolix, vice-everybody
    (& every body's vices).

To die for this!
    After too-numerous appearances:
    Jocose & bellicose, morose
    & gross (that last in the key of D).

But to have lived
    For this: the discoloured,
    Noisome chamberpot attacked
    The olfactory in hospital's portico.

Yes: for this, for these: the least & those
    Gross (in US sense), tearing at your
    Dalmatic to clear tears, noses—meager
    & eager for this folly which is crux.

i.m. John Cardinal O'Connor

The Zen Chapel

All gold
folds like poor
wall
paper.
Temperature
perfect as to not
notice
(yet mention
what's unnoticed).

More, always: never enough thô
grown tired
of contentment-- it was struggle all along
the ancient canal w/ that scent wholly old &
odd
not unlike God
& God I
like you--
Memory's awful when remembrance is gone or
hidden, which is why searching is such
satiety. If I could
see the sky
I'd
see not one dome
but five &
not a cloud in
one. Is that hope
only? If hope
is desire
I hope
never to hope.
Yet to
not hope
is unforgivable
sin,
the Judas sin:

Can't win.
Could lose you, God, mind.
The first two wouldn't mind
nor would I.

Birds guano Saint Theodore till
bronze is white.
Birds cover a woman w/ crumbs
for them.
Ask her to pastel
our
picture
near
the bridge w/out railings,
we're falling
light's failing, grab the flash--
splash!
Come in: water's
warm as sun folds its disk
like a ducat creased on its radius--
for us, the moon is
good silver;
can see a face in its plate.
At night, that moon is just a
White Hole
where all disappears:
gravity's gone with the sun
under cerulean
sky, under water behind
crustationed columns:
no, we never
know anything, that's just reality and
no, never hold hands in a chapel,
which is
why,
at the kiss of peace,
we kiss.

Should old acquaintance
be forgot & never brought
to mind—yes, they should

The Industry of Distraction

More memory
    Of thee
  Or
  For my PC
                  Will not make
          Me
      Happy.

Roundly mocked in a cent-
Refuge of self-deprecation:

Conditional happiness is
Desire in barrister's robes.

The

empty unfolded in

To

vacant store-front

Looks, where a "church"

Once squatted (You'll

Only make it worse, encaged).

By scratching or stratagem, said
"I'll never set foot in that city again".
But that was prior to amputation
& the chalky medication, smarting
Esophagus.

Degrees of misery: pick your
Scale or salver (it can't possibly matter).

Changed names: Veronica,
Give me your linen & I'll
Give you the shroud of Turin.
Be my tabula rasa
Then count me in
As your original sin.

Desire remains, thô the objects
Change: those pewter
Cufflinks, the Florentine sack,
The livid line on the spine's range
Of yer blank, eggshell back.

Love in the absence of touch?

W/out

Your presence, love doesn't feel

like much.

Psittacine shrieks, strident
As sirens come in while all
The time wonder ceases to
Amaze, words to amuse.

Whose voice is whose?
Then a sleep of slate, stabbed
Into strata of lime and shale.
The ivory remains of the whale's
Harpooned backbone, gone.

What are we on/off? Standby?
Stand then & say goodbye.

No one cries, save that garish parrot
On his twisted gibbet, unlaquered—
A mottled bird in motley:
suggests "himself" incessantly.

From A Lost Bus in Jersey

I've renamed "sleep", "work": I'm working
Overtime, and over time I've realized how much
I loathe sleep: the desultory dreams (inexplicable),
the drool staining cheek and pillow; that right
leg-cramp causing the start & jump (making
an ass of oneself in front of a bedded lover).
Then insomnia where strikes were, sleeplessness
like an unproclaimed lay-off w/out being
paid-off; thrill-less pills to kill the ill of unwanted
wakefulness—feckless this is. Joyless sign of newest
sunshine, lambent on the dew-licked power-line
in the fogged back-yard, greyed-in. All night, all
day—even an attempt to rest the restive cells called
"body" by the labour of sleep. Few benefits, but no
sententious cubicled-co-worker—no, I'm not
numbering her stray eyelashes, not counting sheep—
doesn't work, nothing does—but I do: work in sleep.

Le Meridien

Just when you think
You don't know what
You're thinking &
The Venice Glass

Is passed, spuming
& spicèd w/ lant:
this calix drips, rips
lips, palette scourged.

Break the branks
Mister Master fashioned
For your face. Omni-
Everything, I'm not

Fucking kidding—
The subsurface cartograph,
Plastic key, the toll-free cellie,
Yer O/R designer scrubs

Let wear, me (thanks);
Same CD on repeat, room
3416: do not make up
our parlour until

the usurious auto-bar
is empty, loaded towels
in each suite—If you slip
in the shower

or into something more
or less toward naked, I'll
catch you like a cold
before final examination.

Foliage from this vantage—
Can't imagine & forgot
The camera. Who let in
The chimera w/ those

Wind-chimes all the time
In the vacuum, next day
At *Sext,* when every
Benzodiazepine

Was gone and only $
10 between us w/ that
priceless silence and no
tag on commonsense.

At the R, went East, left
You to find on the 1/9
The West Village. Never
To be on the Rialto—

Bric-a-brac brings back
The spectral con-
Sciousness of a browned-
Out memory. Blow

Out the—you know—
Or drip spit
On them
To be certain.

First-lines & Punch-lines

"A priest, a rabbi, and a woman's private parts walk into a bar...

...so the bartender says 'A glass of water? Are you some kind of pussy?'"

"It seems there was this young boy who had a parakeet...

...and the cop says 'Son, that bird done shit and gone.'"

"A Polock finds a lamp with a genie in it...

...and the genie says 'How many lanes do you want on that bridge?'"

"A leggy super-model walks into a blind-man's barbershop...

...and the barber says, 'Well, I guess that explains the beard.'"

"How many ________ does it take to...

...and one to *really* change it."

The Derrick at Rhodia

Below 0 degrees
Under hide's plastic
Dermis, cold as cold-ass
Hatless in thick winter
When wind is itself
A chilled factory
Of open walk-in freezers.
As Atlas' back when
Breeze crept past
Loin-cloth's minor
Cover—Knew it was so
Over when she didn't
Come-- or even call.

Then fall fell fast
Like a fresh soap-cake
In that shower stall:
All those leaves gave
Into gravity's persistence
And in an instant
The host descended into
His goblet.

Say: "Let in the rain
& the child and the spent
Prophet". So they sat,
ate burnt meat from the spit
until the precipitation
doused the open oven.

Oh, when will you ever
Learn? Where there's fire
& a child, the kid gets
burned like a sop to
Moloch in gi-hinnon.

Then there was a message
While I was locked down
Up in the tilted turret, arms
thinning, bruised & hairless.
So I laid down the rifle, a
Mannlicher-Carcano or as
The messenger, only eleven,
Called it, "The enemy's friend".

Smiled at this, turned him
Out of doors, down that set
Of Escheresque steps. Then
Turned the latch shut. I heard
Him shout epithets which hit
Like the popcorn sins
A priest is stoned to death
w/ when he hears First
Confessions. You can call it
Reconciliation, but it's still
Penance.

The message read: "You never
Learned the lesson, though
You sat through the demonstrations,
The remonstrations w/ that
'non-traditional' student we
all hated. But that's not my point,
not my position: if you think it is
then you're mistaken, since I'm
gone for good, I'm as good
as gone & the kid comes with me".

I tore the paper into remains
Of the holes from ticket-stubs that
Drop from the conductor's puncher--
He plays like a musician on the corner.

Sat and then I stood. I sat again
And then stood for good
And took the rifle and took aim

At that running page as he
Sped away from my crooked
Tower: I threw the bolt
Down and blew, very like
A blow-dart into his
Tiny, strawberry heart.

Air: Fin.

Wonder when
You will return
The flights
Have been
Grounded, a weather
System moving
in

On this
wind-day, I am
Not blue
But cold

I could
close
a window

But then
What would
I remember

What would
Bring me to myself?

w/ Sam Turner

IV

July 4

for Seamus Deane & Scott Eden

To me that ceremony is unacceptable: it is not so sane as you imagine. A man who swears before the world to love a woman till death part him and her is sane neither in the opinion of the philosopher who understands what mutability is, nor in the opinion of the man of the world who understands that it is safer to be a witness than an actor in such affairs.

--*Stephen Hero*

Let the dead marry their dead.

--*Ulysses*

He chose his father's birthday, July 4, as the wedding day.

Richard Ellmann, *James Joyce*

I. Gamelios: The Newlydead

Papa go to bed now, it's gettin' late;
Nothing we can say is gonna change anything now;
I'll be leavin' in the mornin' from Kensington Gate,
We wouldn't change this thing even if we could
somehow.

Father's day, wedding day: say
—as quickly and quietly as possible, say
—I do
—I will.

JJ even prays:
—No reporters, no photographers!
No judge in his night-shirt, no priest in his unchaste chasuble
Not even a chapel's bell beating faintly in
Faraway Londowntown...

Innkomes *Evelineing Standard*, snapping this deaded bedlock
On their sidewalking, singing together, hehasher:
Walking by the railing of a path in Kensington
To wax poetworx in museuleum of the Madame:

—You'll never see me there in wax, but in flesh I come,
I draw and take her as (write it, damn you! What else
are you good for): *Wife*—laid down for my friends.

—See: it's a reduncíady. I've known her like the Bible
(I'm writing the sequel). I've died in her, dyed
her with a little cloudy soapy stink of ink, her
flesh a foolscrap: when dried to crust, I've raised
my serif & sealed the unsaid covenantless pact
sinced packed to Pola, Trieste & the rest.

—Damn, Stan: it's a revitition—draped in my habit
of habitchual cunnyoubeall bliss (bless, me father). But
to say I Will will
get her in my will... still I call this A-Marry-Your-Wife
Bill.

—My dame is game for a gamelos: just like Suresee,
sureshe can change like dark mutendlust Shannon
waving godbye to Publin from Canshedung.

NEWSFLESH

We intercorrupt this weldding pome to bring you the lastest from around the glob:
—Wiley Post and Paul Gatty complete round the world flight in record time 80 days 50 hrs and 51 minutes.
—Toscanini refuses to play facist hymn.
Now back to our irregulary scheduled pome, allready in progross.

The Wedding Photo

Arrayed for the bridal, the bride, wiping her eye,
fair creature of trothplight, flapper-hatted, a ewe
'round shoulders (or just a wreath of fleace);
No virgilian white, no forehead seen more fair,

in the darkness of her dress as for a funforall.

Flood-slacked, cane-tapped as third foot; bow-
tied, no tuxego, no wedding banns nor bands
on hands on collars, no priest on leash on leaving
with the

third who walks always bestride them in this still:
the lean solicitor, Munro, coughing.

—Being made riduculus! The waste sad time this is!
        Honey, shall we honeymoan?

Where? Departure desireable to: Stonehenge, Tower
of Lundonne, &
—let me win her in Windsor Forest:
        I need no priest for popery: The muses sit
        sheathed in gossumher, they invite the lay
        with my sylvan maid made wife today:
        Newsrag pictures left my ego bruised
        With this license I wed the world confused.

And then we'll wed
And then we'll bed...

II. Hymenaios: From Noway Pawn

Collect: *Come far away from Galway, laydy*
Yourope's for eloping, gal;
I'm thin, I'm poor, I'm untidy bayby;
Be my muse and I'll be yer Baal.

Versicle: *And when we are married,*
O, how happy we'll be,
For I love sweet Nora, m'lady
And Nora, my lady loves me.

The lovers going through an emblematic ceremony
of throthplight & quick flight to Sceptred Aisle
to Frogland—and then the Blunderer broke:

DAD: sez —And thou shalt eat like those in
flite: with yer loinings girt, biteher herbs,
and blud like a rud rose (or my nose) on sheets
and lintels for proof: I am the Lord of this rooked
and runed castled manouvre, moveover the land
like snakes at the tip of Padric's crozier
slipping lemminglike into Liffey. And I shalt send
playgues one thru ten inclusive reigning katzunddogs
and Frogs from Brittany into Dark Pools, ditch
stagnant and ratty. I am the Lord of this loose
jewel of an eyeal, clipped from diadamn of Angland.
I know all: though thou board the ark alone, my angel
Tom Devin from Heaven tells me you are one to be.
So be it! Away! Anchorites aweigh in sin & cosine
to Angleterrafirmup her Maryage pludge! Thou gyro-
vagues! Thou seraphbaites! Thou shalt see at sea:
Dyoublong is where you belong! I am the Lord
of the Dunce, the Alfa and the Romeo. Ahem, Aman,
Amen!

Poets like trips. Their wives learn to like them, too.
So from Fastasleep Illand they board L'Amore Navicula,
Captain Stooping unwilling to play justusadapax. She, sea-
sick, salt-licked
lips with poetaster on tongue. This over-grown umiak,
amazingon-powered, it seems. So sic she dreams:

After desired departure for honeyluna in
Niagara False (North Armorica), over which
no human had passed with impunity—posing
for a sewveneer photogaffe on The Maidenhead
of the Mist under the Bridel Veil Falls, & another
blackenedwhite in the Cave of the Winds
behind the cataract.

Bridegroom on bridge, perambulates from prow to poop,
cain-thin, bespectled, speculates:
Ecce poor! O, Pater Nosedrunk: Marriage outta mode.

Bridgedroom on bride on mind: pitches bivuovac in slacks
—Eye'll never look back. Nor take a Ringsend
on my fingher: don't need that cataphract,
a vestigal vestal's last link of male to nail me
to the crux of suckramental lust.

And thus, by commodius viscus,
our uncoitussed couple
eleap to Pairus.

Tell no more of emerald ways,
of marriage vows which we see
formalities retarding thee:
My gal, my fair gull calls, prayse—
Moananoning on the waves.

III. Epithalamium: Gausthaus Hoffnung/Dœblin

First he tickled her
Then he patted her
Then he passed the female catheter
--Ulysses

J: An exquisite dulcet epithalame:
—Here Comes Erect & flamey salamie.

N: —O now that I know this fissure
filled for first time with aspic-&-spanked—
O! Love it is a painful case to perform
hymenectomy *sans* ether: break me in
like a new hymnal! Sing your niptuals, taddy:

—For each maiden, shy and nervous,
I do a similar service:
For I detect without surprise
That shadowy beauty in her eyes
The "dare not" of sweet maidenhood
That answers my corruptive "would."

The bridal wind is blowing for love is at his noon
and his first minute after noon, is night.
He felt an unknown and timid pressure, sin's swoon;
She let in the blood-breaking shaft of light:

Bid adieu, adieu, adieu to girlish days!
Her soul unveiled full, shy nakedness;
Are you not tired of your ardent ways?
Finished bestowing your brisk largesse?

—I like a woman to give herself. I like to receive...
—I've given. You've taken: my mambrain is broken. I'm bleedin'...
—Yes: but it could be your boots are too tight?

—(They always want to see a stain in the bed to know you're a virgin): Non, your first and last and have come into your kingdom: long may you rain.

Fordone make we newly thankful!
Allalivial, Allalluvial!
Whorsonnah! Youareah!

—O yes...I was...at the...cha...pel...
—...I...[inaudibly]...I
—O...but you're...ve...ry...wick...ed...

Chamber-potted-meat music in bedpan
daedpan tinking: jiggling furiously allalone
nomore: you are my right hand & my left
knows what you're doing: some Scottish
daunsinge, signifying matrimonie—

> ...whose song is ever
> Epithalamium.
> ...And come into her garden
> And sing at the window,
> Singing: the bridal wind is blowing...

Come: my love, my dove, my beautiful one & sleep.
Though exhausperated, the Daed are my obsession this week.
Do not leave me: your presence makes love grow fonder
And always absence makes the heart go wander.

I lie down in sleep: it comes in a piece:
I lie & write on inside of lids
my nerverending masterbeast:

> In the vague mist of old sounds
> a faint point of light appears:
> the speech of the soul is about
> to be heard. Youth has an end:
> The End Is Here.

Photo by Gabriella Carrizo

Kevin Di Camillo is an award-winning poet, editor, and writer who lives and works in Niagara Falls, New York. He is the author of three previous volumes of poetry, has edited over one-hundred books, and has been anthologized in *Wild Dreams: The Best of Italian-Americana.* His work has appeared in *James Joyce Quarterly, The Antigonish Review, Opium, Daedalus: The Journal of the American Academy of the Arts and Sciences, Prairie Fire, The National Poetry Review, Crisis, Crux, America, Columbia, Soul, The Holy Land Review, Catholic Digest, Publishing Research Quarterly, PublishingPerspectives, The Bend, ArtVoice, Traffic East* and he is a staff-writer for *The National Catholic Register. America Magazine* awarded him the Foley Poetry Prize in 1992, and in 1993 he won the Twin Elms Writers' Center at Princeton's Haiku Award. He is a graduate of The University of Notre Dame and Niagara University, a former Doctoral Fellow at St. John's University, and since 2010 has regularly attended Yale School of Management's Publishing Course. He is a member of The Poetry Society of America, The Academy of American Poets and St. Mark's Poetry Project.

Praise for **Now Chiefly Poetical**

In *Now Chiefly Poetical*, prize-winning poet Kevin Di Camillo has created a new and imaginative mindscape. With amazing verbal agility, he invites his readers to savor the power of his associative designs. Here, verbal dexterity, supported by new forms of evidence, leads to wisdom based on deeply felt polyvalent insights.

—**Patrick Samway, S.J.**, author of *A Publishing Partnership: Flannery O'Connor and Robert Giroux*

"To my ear, Kevin Di Camillo's first book of poetry in nearly two decades brings in the influences of poets as diverse as Louis Zukofsky and Clark Coolidge and Gustav Sobin, among other voices—especially Joyce. *Now Chiefly Poetical* is iconoclastic, abstruse, but also readable and ultimately gives one, to mis-use Barthe's term, 'the pleasure of the text.'"

—**Sam Turner**, four-time winner of The BRIO Prize for Poetry

"With the publication of *Now Chiefly Poetical*, Kevin DiCamillo achieves that rarest of events in American poetry: a uniquely new voice emerges in these poems, a voice rare and refined, thoughtful, reflective--above all, a voice with something important to say to readers who, like many of us, have become overwhelmed with the commonplace and mundane. Like etchings on a Waterford glass, the glint of light caught in his words remind us that poetry *can be, even today*, a thing of beauty and truth."

—**Prof. William Martin, Ph.D.**, Niagara University

“Ritual, 'poetical' language run through a blender and woven into a densely textured fence framing strategic, captivating views of the interior garden.”

—John Slater, O.C.S.O., Abbey of Our Lady of the Genesee
author of *Lean*

“‘Here’s / your sequel to the Bible,’ writes Kevin Di Camillo. No smaller than that claim, *Now Chiefly Poetical,* his collection of verse prayers, blazes bright through the mystic, its muscular music bringing demigods to heel, resting only in contemplation, in liturgies of word that ‘Let in Sun / Let *Vigils* come.’ These poems play sprung staccato, a ‘pugilist’ monk’s rhythm probing words for whispers of clarity. Their well-wrought forms can barely contain the poet’s furious joy in language, his sensual gospel of love.”

—George Guida, Ph.D. Poetry Editor of 2 Bridges Review

23857596R00062

Made in the USA
Columbia, SC
15 August 2018